SPECTRUM®
READERS

MW01047547

THRILLING!
Sports

By Teresa Domnauer

Carson-Dellosa
Publishing

An imprint of Carson-Dellosa Publishing, LLC
P.O. Box 35665
Greensboro, NC 27425-5665

© 2013, Carson-Dellosa Publishing, LLC. Except as permitted under
the United States Copyright Act, no part of this publication may
be reproduced, stored, or distributed in any form or by any means
(mechanically, electronically, recording, etc.) without the prior written
consent of Carson-Dellosa Publishing, LLC. Spectrum is an imprint of
Carson-Dellosa Publishing, LLC.

carsondellosa.com

Printed in the USA. All rights reserved.
ISBN 978-1-62399-156-2

01-002131120

Extreme sports are different from other sports.
The athletes are daring.
They train hard and have special skills.
They do things other people would be
afraid to do.
Extreme sports may look a little wild.
But they are an exciting challenge
for many people around the world.

Skateboarding

Extreme skateboarders like to "get air."
They practice tricks, or stunts, in skate parks.
Skate parks have curved ramps
and smooth bowl-shaped ramps.
Skateboarders zoom up the ramps
and take off into the air.
They fly and flip and twist.
After a jump, a good skateboarder lands on
the board and keeps rolling!

Weird Facts

- You can watch the X Games every year. The X Games are like the Olympics, but for extreme sports.

- In skateboarding, a fall is called a *bail*. Skateboarders wear helmets and pads to protect their bodies.

Snowboarding

Freestyle snowboarders do amazing tricks.
They flip and turn in the air, just like
skateboarders do.
Ski areas have special parks
where snowboarders can practice.
There, they take turns in the halfpipe.
The halfpipe is a valley cut in the snow.
Snowboarders launch high into the air
from the sides of the halfpipe.

Weird Facts

- In 1998, snowboarding became part of the Winter Olympic Games.

- Another kind of snowboarding is called *freeriding*. Freeriders race down steep trails and jump off high mountain cliffs.

Free Skiing

Some skiers ski where no others have before.
These skiers are called *free skiers*.
Some free skiers climb to the top
of jagged mountain peaks.
Others fly to the top in helicopters.
Then, they race down the mountain
at high speeds.
If they come to a cliff, they jump off, land,
and keep going.

Weird Facts

- Free skiers who climb up mountains and then ski down them are called *ski mountaineers*.

- Sometimes, free skiers are up to their hips in powdery snow as they ski!

Surfing

Surfers spend a lot of time in the ocean.
They travel the world looking for
the biggest waves.
Surfers paddle out into the ocean.
When the right wave comes, they "pop up,"
or stand quickly, on their surfboards.
Sometimes, the waves are over ten feet high!
If surfers aren't careful, the waves will
crash over them.
The powerful waves can knock them
under the water.

Weird Facts

- Athletes who ride extremely large, high waves are called *big-wave surfers.* They ride waves over 40 feet high!

- Some of the best places to surf are in Hawaii, Indonesia, Australia, and California.

11

Whitewater Kayaking

Some kayakers paddle in calm lakes or ponds.
Not whitewater kayakers.
They like the thrill of wild,
fast-moving water.
Whitewater kayakers must paddle quickly.
They dodge sharp rocks as rushing water
pushes them downstream.
Whitewater kayakers wear helmets
and life jackets to stay safe.

Weird Facts

- Eskimo first made kayaks from wood and animal bones and skins.

- Kayakers do an "Eskimo roll" if they get stuck upside-down under water. They use their paddles to turn the kayak right side up.

Motocross

Motocross riders do not race on the street.
They race powerful motorcycles
on tough courses made of dirt.
They zoom over hills and through ruts.
They dodge tree stumps and rocks.
They race through muddy puddles.
Motocross racers must be aware of
other riders, too.
Racers don't want to crash into each other.

Weird Facts

- Freestyle motocross riders do tricks in the air, just like skateboarders do. Some can even do back flips!

- To protect their bodies, motocross racers wear special body armor, goggles, and helmets.

BMX

BMX is a short way to say
"bicycle motocross."
Instead of motorcycles,
BMX riders use special bicycles.
Freestyle BMX riders perform stunts.
These riders take to the air.
In skate parks, they launch off ramps.
They bounce off rails.
They fly high through the air and flip.
They land again in the riding position.

Weird Facts

- BMX bikes are smaller and lower than most bikes. They have knobby tires that grip the ground.

- BMX riders wear helmets and pads to protect their bodies in case of falls.

17

Snocross

Some people race snowmobiles.
This sport is called *snocross*.
A lot of snow is needed for snocross racing.
Racers often face heavy snowstorms
that make it hard to see.
A snocross course is icy and bumpy.
The narrow trails twist and turn.
Drivers must steer around huge holes
without crashing.

Weird Facts

- Snocross snowmobiles can go from 0 to 70 miles per hour in about 4 seconds!

- Snowmobiles weigh twice as much as motocross motorcycles. Even so, freestyle snocross drivers can do tricks in the air!

19

Rock Climbing

Rock climbers aren't afraid of heights.
They climb steep rocks.
They move one leg or arm at a time.
Each grip they have on the rock
is called a *hold*.
They test each hold before they move.
Sometimes, rock climbers cannot find a hold.
Then, they must move sideways before they
can go up.
Ropes secure rock climbers in case they fall.

Weird Facts

- Some rock climbers climb without ropes or other people. This is called *free solo climbing*. This can be very dangerous.

- Moving back down a rock using ropes is called *rappelling*.

21

Ice Climbing

Ice climbing is a lot like rock climbing.
But ice climbers face freezing-cold weather.
They scale frozen waterfalls.
They climb big sheets of ice called *glaciers*.
Ice climbers wear spikes on their boots.
The spikes help them grip the ice.
Ice climbers carry special tools, too.
They pound axes into the ice
to help pull themselves up.

Weird Facts

- Ice climbers must not climb when the weather is too warm. The ice gets slippery and can crack!

- Ice climbers wear special clothing that is both warm and waterproof.

23

Skydiving

Skydivers ride high into the air in airplanes.
Then, they jump out!
Skydivers wear parachutes on their backs.
At the right time, they open the parachutes.
The parachutes catch air and let them
float for a while before landing.
Some skydivers jump in a group.
They hold onto each other as they fall.

Weird Facts

- Skydivers always wear two parachutes in case one does not work.

- Skydivers must take lessons on the ground before they go up in a plane.

Bungee Jumping

Bungee jumpers do not jump from planes.
They jump from tall cliffs or high bridges.
Bungee jumpers attach a special cord
to one ankle.
The other end attaches to the cliff or bridge.
A bungee cord is like a big, strong rubber band.
It stretches as the jumper falls.
It is just long enough to keep
the jumper from hitting the ground.

Weird Facts

South Africa has one of the highest bridges
for bungee jumping. It is over 700 feet tall!

A.J. Hackett started one of the first bungee
jumping companies in 1988 in New Zealand.

Sled Dog Racing

In Alaska, sled dog racing is an extreme sport.
The Iditarod is a challenging sled dog race.
The race is about 1,200 miles long.
It usually takes about two weeks to finish.
It passes through frozen, snowy lands.
The racers are called *mushers*.
Each musher leads a team of dogs
that pulls a sled.
The mushers must carry supplies and take
care of the dogs along the tough racing route.

Weird Facts

- The Iditarod race takes about two weeks to finish. It is the longest sled dog race in the world.

- Mushers often put special booties on their dogs' feet to protect them from the cold.

Luge

Luge racers ride on sleds down a track
that is covered with ice.
The track is slippery, and the ride
is windy and cold.
Luge sleds have sharp blades, which make
them very fast.
Luge racers lie on their backs as they slide.
They can't see where they are going!
They steer down the track with their bodies.
Luge racers reach speeds of 80 miles per hour!

Weird Facts

- Luge racers are called *sliders*. They wear helmets and goggles to stay safe.

- There are only a few places in the world that have luge tracks. Lake Placid, New York is home to one of them.

THRILLING! Sports
Comprehension Questions

1. How are extreme sports different from other sports?

2. What do you think it means to "get air"?

3. What is a halfpipe? What extreme sport uses a halfpipe?

4. Where do motocross riders race?

5. What does *BMX* stand for?

6. What is it called when people race snowmobiles?

7. Why do you think rock climbers are not afraid of heights?

8. Why do ice climbers wear spikes on their boots?

9. Why do skydivers wear parachutes on their backs?

10. What is the Iditarod? How long does it usually take to complete?

11. Which of these extreme sports would you most like to try? Which would you least like to try?